117 handy haggling hints

How to negotiate Win, Win, Win deals!

CW01584111

By Peter Thomson
Co-Authored by Derek Arden

Peter Thomson International plc
54 Kenilworth Road . Royal Leamington Spa
Warwickshire . CV32 6YP . United Kingdom

tel +44 (0)1926 339901
fax +44 (0)1926 339139

email: action@pti-worldwide.com
web: www.pti-worldwide.com

117 handy haggling
Hints...How to negotiate Win, Win, Win Deals!

Introduction

There have been many books, tapes and training programmes about negotiation. In fact Adam and Eve were the first people to negotiate and unfortunately they didn't do a very good job of it. The difficulties in getting agreement between people, nations and even religions in the years that followed have caused many conflicts - from family arguments to minor skirmishes - from religious persecution to all out world wars.

In the 21st century - in business, personal and family negotiations there is only one way to negotiate. That's the – Win/Win/Win method. A win for you - a win for the other person and - a win for your joint long term and ever-growing relationship.

To enable this to happen, a great deal of thought and preparation must go into every negotiation - social or commercial. Making the pie bigger for everyone, rather than arguing over the size of the slices. This is the way for everyone to win.

When we decided to write this tips booklet - we did so with one key purpose in mind. To give you, as the reader, a tips booklet containing tried and tested and proven tools that will allow you to create extra income by way of increased sales, increased salary and increased bonuses.

These tools will also enable you to confidently negotiate the price of the myriad of items you buy throughout your life. From the largest purchases such as houses and cars to the smallest items such as a meal for two or even hiring a car.

The ideas in this booklet, when regularly used will increase your personal and business success and wealth. Please do take a moment and let us have any feedback from your actions. We love to keep hearing about your successes.

Take these ideas, practice with them until you fell comfortable and apply them to every area of your life. You'll find that you'll save money, make money and have better relationships.

Every Success

Peter Thomson & Derek Arden

How to use this Tips Booklet

1. Read through the booklet and highlight the actions or methods you are already using.
2. Choose three new actions and test their effectiveness.
3. Listen and watch for feedback from your team. If they spot the changes in your behaviour, you are going too fast!
4. Regularly review this booklet; use it as a self-assessment tool to test further actions/tips. Are there skills you are forgetting to use?
5. The methods are deliberately brief, instant solutions will be found to pressing problems.
6. Some methods are especially lighthearted, all are powerful and practical methods, which will help you, create a style that will suit you and your team.

Every Success

Peter Thomson

Contents

9 **Negotiating Tactics - Theirs**
Things are not always what they seem!

10 **Bargaining Skills**
It's only a bargain - if you wanted to buy it in the first place!

11 **Inventing Solutions**
Every problem has a solution - it takes creative thought to find it!

12 **Confidence**
Fake it - till you make it!

13 **Attitude**
Attitude is everything!

14 **Concluding the Deal**
An order's not an order until the cash is in the bank!

Retail Negotiation

"If you don't ask - they can't say - YES!"

The retail environment is where you can learn and practice many of the skills of negotiation. Lessons learned for a pound can be used to make thousands. Have fun in markets, particularly on holiday - but realise that it's fun with a serious intent. There's seldom anything to lose and much to gain. Just think what a 10% saving on all your purchases would mean over the course of your life. For example if a person's average salary was £50,000 per annum and they saved, by good negotiation, just £5,000 per annum - then - if that sum were invested over a 40-year working life - the payback (Stock Market average return 12% per annum) would be in the region of £4,000,000! Every reason to learn and apply the essential skills of win/win/win negotiation.

1 Always expect to receive a discount - it is seldom that we get a discount if we go into a buying situation not expecting to get one. Be positive you'll be amazed how easy it is when you ask the right questions.

2 Use the authority question - When buying in retail outlets ask the counter assistant "Do you have the authority to give discounts?" If the answer is "yes" you know that discount is available - simply ask "How much can you do this for?" If the answer is "no" ask "Who does?"

3 Deal only with principles - here is a technique to use when house buying or when dealing with any third party or agent. Say to the estate agent "I only deal with principles". When they ask why, respond with "I only deal with someone who is able to negotiate the price. You'll find they'll often respond with "But I can negotiate the price". Then it's up to you - knowing that a reduced price is available.

4 Always ask twice - when buying in a shop and having received the counter assistant's first discounted offer - always ask for a second bite of the cherry. (Particularly if their first offer is stated as a round figure such as 10% or 5%) You know there is more to be had. Say "Surely you can do a little better than that - how much can I have this for?" You'll make them feel better and get a better price for yourself.

5 Use the credit card method - when you know you've reached a point of agreement on price - offer credit card payment or a slightly better price for cash. Retail outlets have to pay the credit card company a percentage of sales when credit cards are used. The retailer will often prefer to give you, the customer, that percentage for a cash deal.

6 Check the paperwork - where retail companies use an order form you'll often find that there is a designated space for - discount. They even put it on the form! If you see that word - make certain you ask "How much discount is available?"

7 Match the price - make sure you do your research as to the other prices that are available in the market place. Many companies will price match other supplier's prices. You simply have to ask: "Will you match your competitors prices?" Then buy from the most reliable supplier.

8 Ask for goods not discount - if a discount isn't available then ask for goods instead. Very often a supplier will be happy to add a bonus item/s rather than lower their price.

9 Ask for the multiple price - in order to find out the lowest price possible ask for a price for a number of items. For example: if you're buying a suit - ask for the price for 5 suits. This will give you an indication as to how low the price could be. Then you may well be able to negotiate that low price for just one suit.

10 Let go emotionally - whilst you have emotion about the buying and selling process - you will not negotiate your best deal. Let go! Realise that there are always other suppliers and always other buyers in the market. Seldom will you have only one choice.

11 Make negotiation fun - particularly in a retail or market environment negotiation should be fun. Negotiate with a smile on your face and make ridiculously low offers as your first proposition. It's almost expected!

12 Learn when the numbers are small - take every opportunity to practice your negotiation skills when the numbers are small. For example - having fun and buying a second hand item in a car-boot sale far below the asking price will be the same mindset and methods used in many of your major negotiation through life. A few pounds saved at the market stall may teach you to save thousand at the board table.

13 Never pay retail - a brilliant question to use is "I never pay retail - is that OK?" Provided that you say this with a smile on your face and in good humour - many retailers will respond with a simple "Yes". Now you can have an easy conversation to provide a win/win/win arrangement.

14 Leave some meat on the bone - always ensure that the other party makes a profit and feels good about the transaction you have struck. If you take all the profit away - you will damage the long-term relationship and may receive both second rate goods and services.

15 Realise it's the process not the price - blunt price negotiation is difficult for everyone concerned. Conversation over a few minutes, building relationship and rapport ensures that everyone walks away smiling. The price is only one factor. People always buy people before they buy the item or its price.

16 Use this fun question in the right situation - here's a question a friend uses to great effect "My partner teaches negotiation - how much shall I tell him I paid?" You realise that this can only be used with a smile and when rapport is high.

Preparation & Planning

"Failing to plan = planning to fail!"

17 Spend ten times more time preparing for your negotiation than the average person. Why? Simply because the average negotiator is totally unprepared at worst, or has spent a few minutes at best. The 6 P's Principle applies: Proper preparation prevents particularly poor performance.

18 Gather every piece of information you can about the other party. This will be available from many sources. People who work with you, customer service staff, previous negotiators – salespeople, press cuttings, Websites, Company Accounts, Other Suppliers, etc.

19 Know who will be at the meeting from the other organisation and find out everything you can about them personally. What is their position in their organisation? What is their authority level? How have they negotiated in the past? Who do you know who has dealt with them before? And what can they tell you?

20 Organise a brainstorming session -get everyone from your team into a room for a brainstorming session. Discuss how the other party negotiates. What are they expecting? How you will respond to any gambits? If you reduce your price what will you trade in its place? How can you increase the benefits for both sides?

21 Sort out all your internal negotiations. Very often the internal negotiations - transfer pricing, credit approval, delivery dates can be more difficult than the negotiations with the customer. Often you will have to go into the internal negotiations in exactly the same way you go into the external negotiations.

22 Review your positions in the preparation stage. Understand your BP (best position), your LP (likely position) and your WAP (walk away position). You also need a FBP – (fall back position) This is the alternative that you have to fall back on, if everything breaks down. Understanding your FBP and how it will affect you makes your negotiating position clearer. Investing the time in having a strong FBP will help enormously.

23 Create an agenda - covering all the points you want to raise – structured in the order you feel will be to your best advantage. Consider sending the agenda to the other side in advance and asking for their comments and additions. This can give you valuable information on their position, their style and the points that are important to them.

24 Role-play the negotiation. Use video feedback. Examine all the issues that might be raised and how you will respond. Use a facilitator who has experience in this type of environment. It can be amazingly helpful in flushing out the difficulties and how you will respond when it is for real.

25 Find out what they want to achieve – they may not want what you want – so it could create a win/win/win relationship just by asking.

Questioning Skills

"The quality of the questions you ask - will determine the quality of the outcomes you achieve!"

26 Use high quality questions. High quality questions are those you've planned in advance structured to meet your objectives. The method to prepare these questions is as follows: Work out the outcome you want - work out the likely answers that will get you that outcome - then work out the questions that will get you those answers. Outcome - answers - questions.

27 Be aware of the questioning/listening ratio - this can be between 2:1 – 4:1 in favour of silence. Remember that you have 2 ears and 2 eyes to listen with and only one mouth to speak with.

28 Consider the use of open questions – closed questions get single word answers or short bursts of information. Open questions enable the other person to expand on their answers - giving you lots of useful information. Use such questions as: Tell me,
how....what....when....who....why.....where.

29 Keep silent once you have asked your question. Remember SILENT is an anagram of LISTEN. You can't listen if you're talking. When you are talking you are giving information and when you are silent you are receiving information.

30 Probe for further information - when your questions haven't solicited all the information you need - keep asking deeper questions until you have everything you require to make a considered judgement.

31 Ask a second time - ask questions again, with different phrasing to make sure you understand the information and the issues correctly. For example: If you've asked what happened after "A" and the answer was - "B" Then next time ask "What happened before "B"? The answer should, of course, be "A".

32 Use appropriate tones of voice - when asking questions use softer tones with harder words and - harder tones with softer words. A forceful question such as "Will you do this?" should be asked with a soft tone of voice. Whereas a soft expression such as "Do you think this would be possible?" should be asked with harder tones.

Listening Skills

"Most people want a good listening to - not a good talking to!"

33 Keep your self-talk at bay - We speak at between 150 and 250 words a minute – yet we can think at well over 2000 words a minute. When you are listening to the words - be careful to make sure your thinking doesn't distract you.

34 Listen with your ears and eyes actively. Active disciplined listening means clearing all the thoughts from your mind and concentrating on what the person is really saying.

35 Make notes - whilst listening let go of thoughts about what and how you are going to respond and just make the odd note about points you want to raise.

36 Have an observer to watch and listen - so they can play back to you what has been said, when you take that all important "Time out" in the negotiations. A second person will bring a new perspective to the negotiation, as they will have picked up signals and information you may have missed.

37 Maintain eye contact – it helps you listen. To keep the other person talking - nod occasionally and respond with "Yes, I see" or "That makes sense". This will keep them positive and keep them talking and giving you vital information.

38 Use the rapid repeat method - this simple yet brilliant technique will improve your concentration and your recall of what's been said. Simply talk along with this other person - in your mind - when they are talking. This repetition of the ideas you're

hearing will hold your concentration at its highest level, as you'll be giving your mind an activity to undertake. It will also enhance your recall of the information you have received.

39 Practice staying - in the now. This is making sure you are concentrating on what is going on at this time – rather than thinking about what happened in the past or what might happen in the future. Police drivers have to take a driving test which shows they are - in the now - all the time - by talking through everything that is happening as they drive their car.

40 Make a record of the key points. Ask permission to make either a written or audio record of the negotiation. Seldom will note-taking be refused.

Body Language - the other person.

"Always believe the Unspoken Truth!"

41 Realise the importance of body language - Body language is the most important aspect in the meaning of communication. American research by Albert Mehrabian shows that, in certain situations, 55% of the information received is through body language, 38% by tone of voice and 7% in the words on their own. Whilst there have been challenges to these figures - within small tolerances - these statistics are correct. Therefore Body Language is a critically important area of negotiation.

42 Evaluate with care - It is 5 times more difficult to lie with body language. Bear this in mind when evaluating the other person's gestures. Remember it is not the single gesture, which counts – a single movement or gesture can be misinterpreted – it is important to take into consideration the clusters of gestures and the circumstances in which they are used.

43 Check for consistency - If you get incongruent body language – go back and check the information you've received by deliberately asking a similar question and then see what reaction and additional information you receive.

44 Rely on the Body Language - When the words conflict with the visual information – almost always rely on the visuals.

45 Take time to read the signals - This may sound obvious but because we get so involved in the detail of the situation we often do not keep eye contact and look at other people. You cannot read the silent language if you do not observe it. Take an observer into the negotiations with you to allow their

right brain to pick up details of the – visual information, feelings and emotions which can be so important. Remember your right brain may almost be shut down with the pressure and concentration that a tough negotiation can create.

46 Spot the more obvious tell tale signals – log them and ask yourself in what context were they used. Analyse the body language signals in the context in which they have been used. Ask yourself questions. Such as: Why did they do that? What did that signal mean? Allow your subconscious mind to provide the answers.

47 Notice any hand to face gestures. These may mean the person using such gestures is either exaggerating or may even be lying. The research that took place in California with nursing staff - showed that when they knew they were *not* telling the truth - there were up to 10 times more hand to face gestures than when they believed they were telling the truth.

48 Observe defensive gestures - such as folding arms, crossing legs or moving away from you. These are gestures that mean the person probably does not agree with you, doesn't like what you are saying and certainly won't be buying - what you're selling.

49 Watch the other person's eyes. Eyes are said to be the windows of the soul and it is very difficult to disguise the meaning that eyes portray. The lyrics from the Eagles famous song says " You can't hide your lying eyes – and your smile is in disguise" It's true! Reports indicate that even the most sophisticated liars, who can manage their body language better than most people - cannot control subtle eye give-aways. We often say " He's a blinking liar" indicating our inherent skill to realise when gestures and eye movements are incongruent with the words being spoken. An increase in the blink rate - has been understood, for centuries to indicate that someone feels under pressure or may even be lying.

50 Watch the pupils - Someone who is excited by a deal or a contract that's in their favour could experience pupil dilation by up to 8 times. Alternatively when people do not like something – their pupils appear to be smaller. Poker players in the western movies always want to wear dark glasses to cover their dilating pupils.

51 Trust your intuition - Remember with raised sensory acuity the average person should be able to operate as effectively as a lie detector. Trust your intuition if you are unsure – your sub-conscious has probably picked something up, below the level of your conscious awareness.

Body Language - Yours

"My Dog Plays Poker"
"Is He Any Good?"
"No Every time He Has A Good Hand He Wags His Tail"
Do you wag your tail?

52 Take care with your first impressions – you only have several seconds to create the impression you want. After 30 seconds it's like quick drying cement. It will take many hours to change that impression. Your handshake is one of the first things that will happen at the meeting – remember that the touch sense, is one of the most powerful senses – check your handshake with a friend to make sure it is achieving the objectives you want to achieve. A neutral handshake always has the hand at 90% to the ground.

53 Change your physiology – to change your mental state. It is well known by NLP (Neuro Linguistic Programming) practitioners that people can change their mental state by just changing their posture. Before your meeting - psyche yourself up – go through a routine of tightening your calves, quads, stomach muscles, squeezing your arms behind your back, tensing your fists, lifting your head as if its on a piece of string – then relax – stand tall, calm and go for it – with confidence and composure

54 Smile – It takes only 14 muscles to smile and a massive - 72 muscles to frown. Smiling breaks down stress and apart from making you feel good – diffuses tension.

55 Relax – if you try too hard to manage your own body language you will leak insincerity. However you need to practice how you respond in those difficult and sometimes challenging situations in the middle of a negotiation. Practice with your video camera and colleagues so you understand how you will be seen by the other party.

56 Be careful where you sit. Across the desk is considered to be very confrontational and therefore a position from which it is much more difficult to gain rapport – influence and persuade. Choose a seating configuration which leads to everybody feeling that they are working together – for a win /win /win solution. For example - sit alongside each other or at a round table.

57 Build rapport by mirroring - match the other person as soon as you meet them. Dress like them, sound like them, use the same words that they do. All this helps to make them know that you are a person with whom they want to do business. And helps you to understand their position – more effectively.

58 Notice your own body language – and adjust it accordingly. Because body language works on a deep level of the sub-conscious mind you will not always be aware of what has happened until after the event. Notice if you suddenly want to cross your arms, rub your nose – fidget in your chair – ask yourself why? Analyse your thoughts and adjust your body language accordingly.

59 Ensure that you look as natural as possible - especially when the pressure is turned up. Avoid fidgeting gestures, hand to facegestures and general unnecessary body language leakage. When an ordinary person is exaggerating / not telling the truth there can be up to 10 times more hand to face gestures.

Creating Empathy

"Good Negotiators have double vision" They can see things from both sides

60 Put yourself in the other person's shoes – look at the situation from their point of view – understand what their objectives are.

61 Ask yourself the question "If I were them – what would be the 10 keys issues for me?" – Put this question at the top of a plain piece of paper and write down the answers as quickly as you can without pausing. Show it to other people involved and ask them to add their thoughts.

62 Observe everything they say carefully - to enable your antennae to see it, hear it, feel it, intuit it from their perspective.

63 Ask others - how they would see it from the other perspective, Remember there are six billion people in the world – everyone different thumb print, eye print, voice print AND perception of the world and what happens.

64 Remember the two young girls - when they were arguing over an orange they finally asked each other why they wanted it – one said "I want the peel to make marmalade" whilst the other admitted she wanted to squeeze it to make orange juice – find out what the other person wants. It may well be that you can both have what you want.

65 Anticipate all their moves - You should not negotiate until you can be certain that you have considered every move the other party is likely to make. Make sure you have checked thoroughly with everyone on your team.

Negotiating Tactics - Yours

"The whole purpose of a negotiating tactic is to change the other person's perception of power"

66 Use time to your benefit - Set time deadlines – 80% of concessions come in the last 20% of the time.

67 Take time outs – adjournments – to talk to your people – defuse the tensions and find out from the people who are not emotionally involved, how they see the situation.

68 Use the power of silence – the benefits of using the power of silence must not be underestimated. Ask pre-planned questions and hold the silence. This is even more difficult on the telephone so discipline yourself to do so.

69 Act smart – play dumb – Dumb is Smart- Generally speaking this works in your favour. Acting too smart and sophisticated breeds competition in a negotiation. People will tell you more if you ask the basic questions even when you think you know the answers. This will let you hear the answers from the "horse's mouth".

70 Set aside issues that cannot be instantly resolved and move on to ones that can be agreed immediately. Take the difficult issues to one side and "park them" to come back to them later. This has the effect of agreeing most of the points and helps the other party come towards an agreement on the outstanding points. They will have invested a great deal of time in the 80%+ of the items which were easy to agree – why jeopardise the deal now.

71 Have price lists – people tend to believe things that are written down. Similarly, write contracts yourself – rather than letting the other party write them – the person who writes the minutes, the contracts - has control.

72 Have a higher authority in your armoury. Average negotiators believe that it is a weakness to have to refer to a higher authority. Experienced negotiators know that having the ability to refer things upward to your "committee" etc can be enormously powerful. It also gives you some thinking time. Make sure it is a committee of people and not one individual.

73 Control your emotions. Act in anger rather than react in anger. After President Krushev of the USSR had banged the table with his shoe at the United Nations in 1967 during a particularly tense part of the debate, the observers were amazed to find, on the video playback that he was still wearing two shoes. He and his team had deliberately bought a shoe for "table banging".

Negotiating Tactics - Theirs

"Things are not always what they seem!"

74 Handle threats in an uncompromising way. Recognise it as a threat to weaken your position and your resolve. Hold a silence. People when they have made a threat expect you to react and the mere fact that you don't do so - often means they qualify what they have said. Many people find this silence very uncomfortable - so make some notes on your pad and then look up and say "That's interesting – Why did you say that?"...or something similar. If necessary take a break, time out or an adjournment as these have the same effect of cooling things down and give you some thinking time. This also gives some quality time with your team to rationally discuss the issues.

75 Never concede to blackmail – you should never deal with people who are unethical. Just as with bullies - if you give in - they see you rewarding bad behaviour which encourages them to do it even more in the future.

76 Make sure you agree - agree the amount of the payment or the concessions up front - as their value will diminish as time passes – when the service has been given. This is similar to the plumber who spends 5 minutes

at your house fixing a leak and then tries to charge you a small fortune. He needs agreement to the price up front while the water is pouring through the ceiling.

77 Understand what liars do – people have different values – some believe it is ethical to tell lies on the basis that the end justifies the means. Having the ability on most occasions to know when people are not telling the truth - can be learnt. For example: When people are in deception mode they generally slow down their gestures, their voice speed. They use less words, have a slight increase in their voice pitch, hold longer eye contact than normal (to compensate for the fact that we generally don't believe people who have shifty eyes) They have more than usual um's and ah's and pause before responding.

78 Be careful about "bugging" - There are usually a number of shops in any major city that sell bugging equipment. You can read where to buy the bugging devices in many magazines. If you are given a specific room or telephone and it doesn't feel right - trust your intuition and go outside and have your conversation in a place of your choosing.

Bargaining Skills

"It's only a bargain if you wanted to buy it in the first place!"

79 Concede reluctantly in small amounts. Make any concession conditional on receiving concessions from the other side.

80 Remember the Magic formula – "If you can do this for us – then we might be able to do this for you". This makes sure you trade concessions and that you put what you want to receive first - and what you are going to give second – remember people focus on the first thing that is said rather than the second thing that is said

81 Price transactions in odd amounts. Odd amounts have more credibility. When figures are precise they have verisimilitude (the appearance of truth) and are regarded as more considered and more calculated.

82 Never accept the first offer - this is a sign of a poor negotiator. It gives the other side the feeling that - they either under priced the transaction - or that they could have obtained other concessions from you. The feeling it creates either at the time or later – when the person has slept on it – is that they can go back and get some more concessions or even abort / sabotage the deal. A good example of this is – if I put my

house on the market today – and someone comes and offers me the asking price – I immediately feel that I have priced the property too cheaply.

83 Avoid splitting the difference - unless that puts you in an advantageous position. The person who offers to split the difference is conceding half of what they originally asked for without trading any concession. It's acceptable to split the difference for small amounts or when there is very little at stake.

84 Aim high – give yourself room to manoeuvre – you can always bring the price down - it is much more difficult and often impossible to increase the price.

85 Soften the blow - When you have to give people bad news – such as a price rise - do this over a long period raising expectations and then offer a slightly lower price than expected.

86 Watch out for the "nibble". This is when things have been agreed and the person asks for something else to get agreement. Children are very good at doing this – they ask for things in small amounts and when they get agreement start asking for additional things. Flag to the other person you understand what is going on by saying, with a smile on your face, something along the lines of "We've worked out a super package for us both, don't spoil it now"

87 Increase the relative value of what you are offering and decrease the relative value of what they are offering you.

88 Use "what if" statements - do this to fact find. This way you will understand what might be acceptable to the other side. However make sure that they fully understand that you are

not making an offer - simply exploring possibilities.

89 Separate the people from the problem. Do not let the issues influence the relationship you've built. Agree that you are both meeting to get agreement to the issue that you both face. Every problem is an opportunity.

90 Don't be afraid to ask. If you don't ask - they can't say "Yes". You'll be surprised when you do ask – how many times you get more than you expected.

91 Have a real walk away position - and be prepared to walk. If you don't have a walk away position - you will leak this information to the other side in your body language.

92 Calculate the real cost of concessions - always calculate based on the profit line not the turnover line. For example if a company usually makes a net profit of say - 10% and a negotiator gives away 5% on a sale - the 5% represents 50% of profit!

Inventing Solutions

"Every problem has a solution - it takes creative thought to find it!"

93 Do things differently. Insanity is doing the same thing over and over again and expecting different results.

94 Take a break, use your imagination - relax – go to that balcony overlooking the sea, take in fresh air, smell the ozone, look at the horizon – get the big picture.

95 Brainstorm the issues - have creative sessions with colleagues who are involved in the negotiation and with those who have no part to play. They will see things from a different perspective.

96 Access your right brain – write focused questions about your negotiations (style, content etc) on a piece of paper/book and keep it with you. The answers will come to you when you least expect them. Einstein got his ideas for the theory of relativity when he was sitting on a grassy knoll. Edison found most of the solutions to his unsolved experiments when he was meditating. Always keep a book with you to write down the ideas when they come to you at those unexpected moments.

97 Involve advisors and coaches – the time spent trying to see how the pie can be increased for everyone is time well spent. Coming up with alternatives can be productive for you and your organisation – seek solutions that create agreement rather than conflict.

98 Use a facilitator - sit down with the other side and with a mutually agreed facilitator to help you jointly find solutions to the problems.

Mediators do this in a more structured way when negotiations have broken down – often keeping both parties, who by this time are in conflict, in separate rooms and moving between those rooms exploring the options.

99 Look outside the box. Remember the 9 Dots problem. Where you have 9 dots in a square, you have to join them with 4 straight lines without taking your pen off the paper. Everyone assumes they can't go outside the box, and of course that is one of the ways to do it. Find creative solutions.

Confidence

"Fake it - till you make it!"

100 Ensure you dress for success – make certain that you look the part. Dress appropriately to the people, the situation and the issues. If you are involved in a business negotiation - wear a smart business suit, shiny shoes - be as smart as possible. It will reflect on your results. If you're negotiating with people who are usually more casually dressed - match that style.

101 Practice constantly - practice your negotiation skills wherever possible. Negotiation on the price of a meal will stand you in good stead when you're negotiating for thousands or millions. Constant practice will make you a professional. After all - amateurs practice until they get it right - professionals practice until they cannot get it wrong.

102 Look and sound confident - the way you walk into the negotiating arena will have a major impact on the other party. Walk with confidence - speak with confidence and you'll be confident. Fake it till you make it!

103 Keep everything neat and tidy - a neat briefcase and well-presented paperwork will add to your confidence. It looks as though you are in control of yourself and the situation.

Attitude

"Attitude is Everything!"

104 Maintain a positive win/win/win attitude - your attitude at the start of the negotiation will have a major impact on the results you achieve. People like to deal with others who have a positive attitude to life and to business. You'll make it easier for everyone to talk and concede in an atmosphere of positivity.

105 Psyche up before you start - get in the mood for negotiation before you negotiate. Take some time on your own and get your thought process running in the appropriate mode. A series of spoken "yes's" will get you into "yes" mode ready for anything that happens.

106 Maintain your energy level - ensure that you eat and drink the right foods and liquids. Excess coffee or tea or eating chocolate will reduce your energy level. Eat fruit and drink water particularly if you are likely to be involved in a meeting/ negotiation that will take place over a number of hours.

107 Use positive language - it is far easier for people to understand what you're saying if you phrase your words in positive

language. Avoid the use of linguistic negative such as - don't, can't etc.

108 Re-frame unhelpful comments - when the other party makes a negative statement - reframe it by asking "Do you mean ... and phrasing it in positive language" After all, every problem is an opportunity, one man's meat is another man's poison and the glass can either be half full or half empty!"

109 Make certain your self talk is positive - ensure that the words you say inside your mind are focusing on a positive outcome and positive process. Eradicate any negative doubts and thoughts as they will damage your external language patterns and subsequently damage your results.

Concluding the Deal

"An order's not an order till the cash is in the bank!"

110 Always ask for the order - when you are the seller in a negotiation - do not leave without asking for the order. You've put in the hard work now is the time to reap your just rewards. A simple "Shall we go ahead then?" may be all you need. Whichever words you use to ask that closing question - make certain you do!

111 Suggest an alternative - one of the oldest and most honest ways to close a transaction is to suggest an alternative. Would you like the red one or the blue one? This assumes the conclusion of the deal and offers a simple alternative.

112 Enough is usually enough! - here is a simple question you can use to conclude a deal. "Will 3 be enough?" If the answer is "yes" your customer wants 3. If the answer is "no" your customer wants more than 3!

113 Use the tin-cup method - get colleagues or other people to support your cause before asking for the final agreement. This is known as "tin-cupping" getting other names in the "cup" before you make your proposition.

114 Close on a minor point - if someone agrees to a minor point of the transaction they are in effect agreeing to the whole transaction. For example: "Do you want a balcony and sea view?" If this question is answered with a "yes" then the person is then highly unlikely to refuse to book the holiday.

115 Close early in the conversation - it's never too soon to test close to find out the real intent of the other party. Such questions as: "Does this make sense so far?" or "Is this OK with you?" "Does this sound good?" "Does this look right?" would be ideal test closes.

116 Leave when the deal is done - once the agreement has been reached do not spend too much time socialising. Sign the papers, thank the other party for their agreement, shake hands and . . . go! Any excess conversation after agreement has been reached may make the other party re-consider their options and your position.

117 Don't celebrate too enthusiastically - if you are too enthusiastic the other side will believe that they struck the wrong deal. Be happy but not too happy!

Conclusion

In negotiation, as in life, nothing works every single time. Take each of these ideas and test them. Find out which work best for you and your preferred style. Then practice until you can use them almost without conscious thought. Prepare for every negotiation thoroughly, be professional in your thoughts and actions and maintain a positive win/win/win attitude throughout. In this way you will be certain to gain the respect of your colleagues, customers and suppliers and be certain to win the negotiating game more often than ever before.

Good luck!
Peter Thomson and Derek Arden

Derek Arden

Biography:

Derek Arden is now one of the U.K.'s Leading management consultants on Negotiations, Influencing and Persuasion. He runs his own company that provides specific targeted consultancy, training and coaching. His advanced Negotiation Skills and Relationship Management Workshops are very successful and used by many large companies and several business schools.

A qualified banker and formerly a Director of Multi-National Relationship Banking with the leading UK financial services group. In that role he led many large and complex negotiations - highlighted by the financing of the Great Universal Stores hostile acquisition of Argos and the Granada takeover of Forte.

Derek is a lecturer at the International Business School "Henley Management College" as well as being a visiting speaker at Durham University Business School and the University of Surrey.

A member of the Professional Speakers Association - a sought after keynote speaker at seminars and conferences.

A licensed Neuro-Linguistic Programming Business Practitioner. A fellow of the Chartered Institute of Bankers, a fellow of the Institute of Management and a member of the Institute of Directors.

Peter Thomson

Biography.

Peter Thomson is now regarded as the UK's leading strategist on personal and business growth. Starting in business in 1972 he built 3 successful companies – selling the last to a public company, after only 5 years trading, enabling him to retire at age 42.

Peter is now Chairman of Peter Thomson International plc and spends his time sharing his proven methods for business and personal success via audio and video programmes, books, seminars and conference speeches.

With over 60 audio programmes written and recorded he is Nightingale Conant's leading UK author.

Peter is the publisher, writer and presenter of the widely acclaimed personal development audio newsletter "The Achievers Edge!" And "The Accelerated Business Growth System"- a monthly CD Video, CD Audio and Action Planner. He is also the author of tgiMondays PLUS - a weekly Motivational Monday Message - Monthly Audio CD - Quarterly Book and Yearly Telephone Seminar.

The American Intercontinental University in London – with permission granted by the American Government - awarded Peter an Honorary Doctorate (Doctor of Letters) for his work in communication skills and helping others to succeed in life.

As a family man (4 sons), 30 years of business experience on his own account and as a keen golfer his presentations and audio works are brought to life with true stories of success and failure - designed and delivered to make any listener realise that they too can achieve their goals, be more successful and live the life they want!

A hallmark of Peter's work is his use of thought-provoking original expressions - expressions that stop people in their mental tracks and have them re– evaluate their beliefs about success.

"People will never consistently do - who they aren't!"

"Better the right "no" answer than the wrong "yes" answer!"

"Most people never ask you the real question - they ask a question about the wrong answer!"

"Ask yourself the *EASY* questions and you'll have a *HARD* life, ask yourself the *HARD* questions and you'll have an *EASY* life!"

"Time and distance travelled compounds the effect of error!"

"If it's too easy you don't care to try - if it's too hard you don't dare to try!"

"In a world where the big things make little difference - it's the LITTLE things that make a BIG difference!"

20 Tips to Promote you and your Business with Booklets!

(They can even be customised for you)

1. Send this booklet to your customers at year's end, thanking them for their business.
2. Use this booklet as a "thank you" for a sales appointment.
3. Mail this booklet to your prospect list to stay in touch with them.
4. Offer this booklet free with any purchase during a specific time, with a certain purchase amount, or when opening a new account.
5. Distribute this booklet to prospects at a trade show.
6. Give this booklet as an incentive for completing a questionnaire or survey.
7. Include this booklet as a "thank you" gift when mailing your invoices.
8. Package this booklet as a value-added bonus with a product you sell.
9. Deliver a copy of this booklet to the hands of the first "X" number of people who enter a draw or come to your store.
10. Provide copies of this booklet to people and organisations who can refer business to you.

11 Give the booklet away at a trade fair or exhibition to attract more potential customers to your stand

12 Give a Tips Booklet as an incentive for completing a Customer Survey Form

13 Include a Tips Booklet as a "Thank You" for the order when sending an invoice or statement

14 Bundle or package a Tips Booklet as a value added bonus for ordering a particular product from your range

15 Send an appropriate Tips Booklet to your staff as a reminder of some of the key principles of success - or as a thank you for a job well done

16 Use packs of Tips Booklets as prizes in a raffle or charity appeal

17 Give a Tips Booklet to the first 50 people who come to your shop or business

18 Use a Tips Booklet as a bonus for sponsorship activation

19 Use a Tips Booklet to launch a new product - including product details in the centre pages of the booklet

20 Use a Tips Booklet as a memorable Change of Address card

Other Booklets in the Series...

"117 Ways to get Almost Anyone to do Almost Anything!"

by Peter Thomson

"117 Ways to Grab Your Life by the Throat and Really Make it Happen!"

by Peter Thomson

"117 Ways to get Your Audience To Shout More, More, More Every Time You Stand and Speak!"

by Peter Thomson

"117 Ways to Motivate Your Team Without Breaking the Bank!"

by Sharon Thomson

"How to get 1000's of Leads for Free!"

by Peter Thomson

Notes

Notes